COACHING

FOR

RESULTS

Transforming Managers from Bosses to Coaches

By Rich Meiss - M.B.A

D1367271

Title: **Coaching for Results**

Subtitle: **Transforming Managers from Bosses to Coaches**

Author: Rich Meiss – M.B.A

Description: This book is for the leader, manager, supervisor or coach who wants to fully develop his/her people while getting great business results. Included are specific word tracks and ideas that can be used to handle five different coaching situations including 1) reinforcing good behavior, 2) redirecting poor behavior, 3) addressing bad habits, 4) confronting poor performance, and 5) facilitating conflict resolution between employees. Also included are specific ideas for building three key coaching skills: 1) asking good coaching questions, 2) listening and communicating effectively, and 3) giving effective feedback. Readers will discover a wealth of ideas related to coaching's basic tenet: growing people while getting great results.

Printed in the United States of America

Published by:

MEI Press
Minneapolis, Minnesota
Meiss Education Institute
7300 Highway 7
Excelsior, MN 55331
Phone: 952-446-1586
www.MeissEducation.com

ISBN-13: 978-1475240450   ISBN-10: 1475240457

:

INTRODUCTION AND WELCOME

How we define coaching in this book

If you used the word *coach* as little as 10–15 years ago, most people would equate that with some type of athletic, artistic or educational endeavor. A person who utilized a coach was probably an aspiring athlete, artist or student looking to improve his/her game, performance or grades. In fact, the *American Heritage Dictionary* defines *coaching* this way: "A person who trains athletes or athletic teams; a person who gives instruction, as in singing or acting; a private tutor employed to prepare a student for an examination."

Before the 21st century, the word, *coaching,* was not used much in the business world. But what a difference 10 or 15 years makes! Google the words "Coaching Organization" today and you will find over 6,500,000 matches. Coaching organizations and businesses have grown faster than green grass on a warm day after a Minnesota spring rain. Much is being written in the world of business about coaching, and most of us probably know someone who in recent years has developed a business as a life coach or executive coach. Because this term is relatively new and carries so many different meanings, let's narrow its definition and scope in light of this book.

Ask any 10 professional coaches their definition of coaching, and you'll probably get at least 10 different definitions. Yet all would probably agree coaching contains most of these elements:

- It is a dialogue of some sort — either face to face, by phone or by electronic communication.

- It is generally a one-to-one relationship.

- It usually involves observing behavior and giving feedback to the coachee.

- It is primarily designed to help the coachee learn, grow, perform and get better results.

- It has as its end goal the accomplishment of personal and/or professional goals.

Madeline Homan and Linda Miller sum it up well with their definition in their new book, *Coaching in Organizations*: **"Coaching is a deliberate process using focused conversations to create an environment for growth, purposeful action, and sustained improvement."**

There are many different kinds of coaching being used in organizations today. Here is what this book is *not* about. It is not specifically aimed at Life Coaching (helping individuals achieve personal goals) or Executive Coaching (preparing business leaders for career growth). It *is* aimed at Performance Coaching (showing managers how to help their individual contributors grow and achieve enhanced performance). Note that the aim is twofold: 1) the growth of the individual, and 2) the accomplishment of better results. In simple terms, the aim of Coaching for Results is "growing people — getting results!"

The emphasis of this book, then, is helping internal managers, supervisors and other "people leaders" become effective in the roles of, and skills of, a great coach. While many organizations are hiring outside coaches to help their people, the premise of this book is that significant growth and development, and enhanced results can be obtained by training internal managers to be effective coaches for their direct reports. That's the purpose of this work. Enjoy learning about Coaching for Results!

About the Author

Rich Meiss – M.B.A.

Meiss Education Institute

Rich Meiss has played a key role in the development of people since 1972, holding executive positions with Personal Dynamics Institute, Carlson Learning Company, The Bob Pike Group, and now president of Meiss Education Institute.

Rich has personally trained over 65,000 trainers, presenters, employees and leaders, conducting workshops and seminars in over 150 cities in the United States, Canada, Mexico, Europe, Asia and Africa.

Rich works with organizations in creating and delivering innovative training programs at the organization level (coaching, team building, sales, service), at the personal level (leadership, empowerment, motivation) and in train-the-trainer/facilitator workshops. Rich easily warms up to his audience and is known for his ability to involve and engage participants through his interactive presentations and seminars.

An inspiring speaker and trainer, Rich delivers workshops, keynote presentations and seminars each year to businesses, organizations and trade associations. His topics vary, but his theme always centers on increasing personal and organizational productivity through developing the human side of enterprise. Rich is an active member of the American Society for Training and Development, and he addresses his peers often at national conferences. He has a B.A. in Education from the University of Minnesota, and an M.B.A. from the Ken Blanchard College of Business at Grand Canyon University.

Special recognition includes being listed in Who's Who in the Midwest and Emerging Leaders in America.

Rich is the author of four other books including *Gifts: Ideas to Enhance Results at Work; How to Design and Deliver Powerful Presentations; SCORE! Super Closers, Openers, Reviews and Energizers for Enhanced Training Results; and SCORE! Two More Super Closers, Openers, Reviews and Energizers for Enhanced Training Results.*

Meiss Education Institute is a training, speaking, and consulting firm that specializes in helping organizations capitalize on their human resources.

Seminars and keynote topics include the following:

Adventures in Attitudes: *A Guided Program for Achieving Personal and Professional Success*

Building Professional Communication Skills: *Improve Communications, Build Positive Work Relationships, and Increase Organizational Effectiveness*

Coaching for Results: *Growing People ...Getting Results*

Consultative Selling Skills: *Creating Your Competitive Edge*

Creating High-Performing Teams: *Improve Performance, Increase Productivity, Foster Teamwork, and Create Positive Change within the Organization*

High-Impact Presentations: *Putting Punch Power & Pizzazz into Your Presentations*

Lead Like Jesus: *Lessons from the Greatest Leadership Role Model of All Time*

Making Meetings Work: *Learn to Lead and Facilitate Effective Meetings*

World-Class Service: *Deliver Service That Exceeds Your Customers' Expectations*

Invite Rich Meiss to present at your conference, training, staff development or professional development session. Rich is also available for keynotes, conference breakouts and workshops. Call or e-mail for more information.

Meiss Education Institute

866-446-1586 toll free

952-446-1586 Twin Cities

rich@MeissEducation.com

Rich Meiss

TABLE OF CONTENTS

Rich Meiss

COACHING

FOR

RESULTS

CHAPTER 1

Coaching for Results:
The Overview

One of the most pressing challenges facing organizations in America today is finding and keeping talented people. All the data point to the fact that we are in an era where there are more jobs than there are skilled people to fill those jobs. Our talent pool is shrinking! It's not that we don't have enough people to fill the jobs — we just don't have the right match of skilled, intelligent people who can keep us competitive in today's marketplace.

With such a short supply of good people, an important task for managers and leaders is to learn how to develop their people to their full potential. That is the purpose of this book on Coaching for Results. We define coaching as a series of meaningful conversations designed to grow people while getting results. Notice that coaching is a balance of getting results while helping people grow. Few people will have the opportunity to fully develop their potential without the help of a competent and caring coach. And that is becoming the role of more and more managers today — learning how to coach their people. Just as an athletic coach works to bring out the best in his/her team members, managers in organizations today need to learn how to coach and develop their people.

From Boss to Coach

Although some organizations today have made the leap from the old-style "command and control" type of organizational model, many managers still rely on this method. And let's be honest about it: it's rather compelling to become the boss, isn't it? When we finally reach that goal of becoming a "person in charge," it feels like we've earned the right to be in charge. We've paid our dues. We've worked hard for this promotion, and now everybody else had better do what we want them to do! We begin to develop the habits of "being the boss" that we've seen modeled by others above us.

This approach to managing has worked well for the U.S. military and in some organizational cultures where there is little to no change going on. It works when you only want people to salute and do exactly what you've asked them to do. While it may work in the short term, it is shortsighted in most organizational cultures today. Most workers want to be treated like human beings, not machines. They resent being pushed and prodded, with no input into the direction of the team or the decisions being made. They want a manager who understands the importance of helping them grow while they get the needed results.

Although this is a bit simplistic, here is a summary of the differences between being a coach and a boss:

Coaching	Bossing
Leading and inspiring	Dictating and controlling
Asking and listening	Telling and directing
Seeks the answers	Knows the answers
Goal driven	Process driven
Future oriented	Past/present oriented
Customer/people focused	Systems/process focused
Setting direction	Setting plans and rules
Empowering	Controlling
Looks for solutions	Looks for problems/blame
Seeing people as they could be	Seeing people as they are

Bosses often have a philosophy about people that says they are lazy and need to be "motivated." They need to be poked and prodded to get things done. They use the old "carrot and stick" philosophy, appealing to reward or fear. Bosses believe they know the answers to issues and problems, and that their people should listen to them and comply with their requests. They generally try to solve all the problems and make all the decisions themselves, missing out on the input of their people. Bosses tend to talk at people, directing and controlling.

Coaches tend to operate with a philosophy about people that says most people want to be effective and productive, and they often need someone to challenge them and encourage them along the way.

Coaches believe that:

- You can't motivate people. People are already motivated (but for their own reasons).

- You can create an environment in which people motivate themselves (when you tap into their reasons).

- The way you create a motivational environment is to understand the needs and values of people, and meet those needs and reinforce those values in the workplace.

- The most satisfying and productive relationships are authentic.

- In authentic relationships, people are free to say what's on their minds — the thinking and saying gaps are small. Open communication is common and encouraged.

- People grow best when a competent and caring coach helps them see the impact of their behaviors.

The 4 G Coaching Model

To help people become great coaches, remember the 4 G model.

The four G's are Good/Goal, Gap, Guidance and Growth, illustrated as follows.

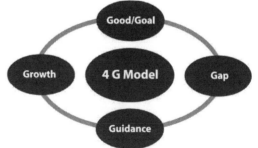

Strong coaches start out by identifying the "good." They personally take the responsibility to set the values, purpose and vision of their enterprise. They set standards and ask people to abide by these standards. Excellent managers also always coach to the highest good. By doing so, they help keep their organizations from experiencing some of the ethical lapses that have dogged many in the past decade — the Enrons and WorldComs and Arthur Andersons of the world. Those organizations got caught in the trap of managing by objectives rather than managing by values. Strong coaches manage by values.

Once the highest good is established, coaches need to identify the specific goals they'd like to reach — for each individual contributor, as well as for the overall department or organization. Good coaches recognize the need of most people to be involved in setting goals, so they allow employee input into the process. This process helps build a spirit of "individual responsibility" so often missing in organizations today. When participants believe they have a say in what is to be accomplished, they tend to be more accountable for their actions and behavior. Together with the individual contributor, good coaches come up with a set of SMART goals for each person, as well as for the department and/or organization.

Specific	Goals should be specific.
Measurable	Goals need some metrics to measure progress.
Actionable	Goals should be action-oriented.
Responsibility Assigned	Goals should be assigned to an individual or team member for accountability purposes.
Time-Specific	Goals should have a time element for completion.

After establishing the "good" and the "goals," coaches look for gaps in performance. They start by asking the team member for their input on how things are going. They ask what successes the team member is having, and what specific strategies led to those successes. They also ask what developmental areas their people want to work on. Good coaches listen without interruption. They ask focused, open-ended questions to pull out as much information from the team member as possible. After listening, they present their feedback and ideas. They point out both positive gaps and negative gaps. If there is a positive gap (the contributor is performing *above* the level of the good or the goals), the coach looks for ways to specifically praise the performance.

If there is a negative gap (the contributor is performing *below* the level of the good or the goals), the coach looks to redirect the performance back to good. Good/goals and gap make up the first two G's.

Giving proper guidance, the third G of the formula, makes up the majority of the content in the book. Effective coaches identify what kind of guidance is necessary to close the gaps in the good and the goals, and they fulfill the following three roles and two special situations of an effective coach.

The coach as Confidant: becoming a guide to help team members work through issues. (Chapter Two)

The coach as Cheerleader: praising good performance when it is delivered. (Chapter Six)

The coach as Corrector: redirecting poor performance to a better outcome. (Chapter Seven)

The coach in special situations - **Coach as Challenger**: confronting continued poor performance, and **Coach as Facilitator**: working out tough issues between employees. (Chapter Eight)

The final G of the model is Growth. Good coaches are devoted to not only getting results, but also helping their people grow. This is usually done through the process of mentoring people by using three fundamental coaching skills. These skills include asking good questions, listening effectively, and then giving balanced feedback. Chapters Three through Five go into significant detail on these fundamental coaching skills.

Growth in people also happens as coaches strive to walk the fine line between being sensitive to people and being focused on goal achievement. This concept of people focus vs. production focus has been written about in management literature for many years, first made popular by Robert Blake and Jane Mouton in their **Managerial Grid Model** (1964), and later expanded on by Paul Hersey and Ken Blanchard in their **Situational Leadership Model** (1969). The basis of these models is that some managers or leaders (coaches) are more concerned about people (or supportive behavior), and others are more concerned about production (or directive behavior). Good coaches maintain a balance in both of these factors — people and productivity.

The balanced model can be shown in this way:

PEOPLE FOCUS	High people focus Low productivity focus	High people focus High productivity focus
	Low people focus Low productivity focus	Low people focus High productivity focus

PRODUCTIVITY FOCUS

To do a quick check of your tendency to fit into one of these quadrants, spend a few minutes going through the list of tendencies on the next page, and honestly assess your coaching style characteristics.

Coaching Style Characteristics Checklist:

In the chart below, check those characteristics that are generally true of you as a manager, leader and coach. You may have some check marks in all the quadrants.

___Avoid confrontation	___Build people
___Difficulty making decisions	___Clarity of purpose/goals
___Fear loss of approval	___Decisive
___Fun loving	___Energetic
___Listen selectively	___Good listener
___Low assertiveness	___Highly intuitive
___Low goal directedness	___Highly responsible
___Loyal	___Lead by example
___Need approval of others	___Results & people oriented
___Relationship driven	___Self-confident
___Sincere and caring	___Values driven
___Social, amiable	___Solve problems
___Avoid accountability	___Assertive
___Avoid confrontation	___Autocratic, confrontational
___Avoid focus on results	___Fear loss of power
___Indecisive	___Focused on personal goals
___Low energy	___High energy
___Not assertive	___Highly responsive
___Not creative	___Insensitive to people
___Process focused	___Overly confident/arrogant
___Seek security	___Poor listener
___Swayed by others	___Results oriented
___Unclear goals	___Self-focused
___Weak initiative	___Very decisive

By examining the quadrant where most of your check marks were located, you can get a sense of your tendency to be either more supportive and people focused (upper left), more directive and productivity focused (lower right), both people and productivity focused (upper right), or neither people focused or productivity focused (lower left).

Here are some general truths about the model:

1. Most coaches will have some tendencies in all of these quadrants but will fit more naturally into one of the quadrants.

2. The goal of the model is to strive for the upper right-hand quadrant, which shows a balance between people and productivity.

3. Most of us will have to work hard to maintain this balance.

Chapter Seven in this book will give you more ideas about your specific behavioral style tendencies, and how your style impacts this people/productivity model. You'll also gain some ideas on how to create more of a balance between people and productivity, relationships and tasks. By studying and applying these concepts, coaches will be prepared to fulfill the 4th G of the model — helping their people grow.

The 4 G model of Good/Goal, Gap, Guidance and Growth can lead you to greener pastures in getting results while you grow your people. If you are looking for ways to help your people — or yourself — to become better coaches, continue reading the chapters in this book. You might find that these ideas will help your organization solve one of its most difficult issues of the next decade and beyond — developing and keeping good employees!

CHAPTER 2

The Coach as Confidant:

Becoming a Mentor

Have you ever had a special person in your life who saw more in you than you saw in yourself? I've had several of these people in my life. The first was my high school German teacher, Frau Schmidt. She challenged me to get outside of my comfort zone by suggesting that I set a goal to travel to Europe after I graduated from college. Her passion was helping students learn about the languages and customs of other cultures. Because of her, I traveled to 13 different countries in Europe the year I graduated from college, and greatly expanded my horizons.

Another person who had a profound effect on my life was my Dale Carnegie Course instructor, Sam Carlson. When I was a sophomore in college, my father enrolled me in the Dale Carnegie Course in Morris, Minnesota. I was 19 at the time, and a pretty shy Midwestern farm boy. It was in that course that I got the vision to become a public speaker and trainer, and that vision set the course for my life's work. At the graduation session of the class, Sam Carlson challenged me by saying, "Rich, when you become 30 years of age, look me up, because I think you would make a great Dale Carnegie instructor!" In less than two years from that moment, I was working with Sam to set up and help conduct Dale Carnegie Courses. And that momentum launched a 30+ year career in speaking and training.

Who was that person in your life who caused you to see a bigger picture of yourself and your future? Was it a parent, a friend, a spouse, a partner, a boss, a teacher or a colleague? Regardless of the role this person played, he/she became a mentor, right? In essence, he/she was a coach — a confidant!

We have defined coaching as a series of meaningful conversations designed to grow people while getting results. Most of the time when someone talks about a coach, he/she is referring to someone who stands beside him/her to help him/her get better results in his/her life. In the classic sense, this is someone who becomes a "guide on the side," a mentor who helps another person work through his/her own problems, make his/her own decisions, or reach his/her own goals. This is not a classic "fix-it" person or "answer" person. He/she is a guide or a confidant.

Effective coaches/confidants have high expectations of their people.

The confidant sees something in us that we don't see in ourselves. They have high expectations of us and often help us rise to the level of these expectations. This is called the Pygmalion Effect — named after the play (*Pygmalion*) about Professor Higgins and Eliza Doolittle. Professor Higgins makes a bet that he can teach a poor flower girl to speak and act like a lady — and he makes good on his bet. Eliza becomes a polished English lady.

Studies by Robert Rosenthal and Lenore Jacobsen proved the truth of this Pygmalion Effect on school students in the classroom.

In their study, they showed that if teachers were led to expect enhanced performance from some children, then the children often did show that enhancement. In some cases such improvement was about twice that shown by other children in the same class. Similarly, studies by the Gallup Organization have shown that employees respond to the encouragement and appreciation shown them by their immediate manager.

Think of the impact you have on the people whom you coach — whether you are their parent, teacher, colleague or manager. What are your expectations of your higher performers? You probably communicate those expectations to them through a combination of words and nonverbal communications. And in the same way, you communicate lower expectations to your lower performers. So raise your level of expectations and communicate that to those lower performers. Communicate in your words and your body language how much you believe in them. Let them know that you are there for them. One of the ways that you do that is through the way you ask questions and listen to them.

The tools of a master confidant are communication tools.

These tools include asking effective questions, listening actively and giving balanced feedback. Believing that most often "the answers to a person's dilemma are within that person," the master coach uses these communication tools to assist his/her team member in digging deep within to discover the answers needed. Let's examine this coaching tool chest in more detail.

The first tool of the coach as confidant is asking positive questions.

Most coaches today are still locked in the old "problem-solving" mode of thinking. They ask negative questions, such as "What's wrong with you — why can't you perform at a higher level? When will you ever get it right? Whose fault is it that you are performing this way?" These negative, "problem focused" questions cause people to become defensive and give up. They cause people to shrivel up and die rather than grow and flourish.

Good coaches use positive questions such as "What do you really, really want? What will it take for you to get it? What resources are available to you to help you accomplish your goal? What would need to exist for you to produce at the level you'd like and achieve the goals that you want to reach?"

These kinds of positive, "solution-focused" questions bring out the best in people. They cause people to find the answers within themselves, and then rise up and meet the challenge. They are positive, motivating questions!

Solution-Focused Questions	vs.	Problem-Focused Questions
What do you really want?		What's wrong?
When do you want it?		Why did this happen?
How might you get it?		Whose fault is this?
What resources are available?		Why can't you succeed?

Think about the questions you are asking the people whom you coach. Make your questions forward thinking (solution focused) rather than backward thinking (problem focused).

Start your questions with the positive words "what" or "how" more often than with the negative words "why" or "who." Get your people thinking about the possibilities of the situation vs. the problems of the situation.

A second tool of the coach as confidant is being an effective listener.

Great confidants know that most of the time, the answers that a team member is looking for reside within them. After asking a good question, they become quiet and listen. And they listen actively. They encourage their team member with positive body language, such as nodding the head and smiling. They use verbal encouragers such as "Oh, I see" and "That's interesting." They encourage the person to continue talking by phrasing good solution-focused questions, starting with the words "what" and "how."

17

Good listeners also recognize the power of voice tone and nonverbal communications. They believe that more is being said by the tone of voice and the nonverbal communications than by the words that are being used. They learn to "listen between the lines" to the tone, gestures and body movements of the other person.

And they use these clues to help the person get a sense of what they are really saying by paraphrasing, playing back what they see and hear. "So I hear you suggesting that..." and "It seems to me that what you are thinking is..." are thought starters that the coach uses to continue the conversation. And they always confirm their hunches by asking something like "Is that what you are saying/feeling/thinking?"

Through this process of asking good questions and listening, effective coaches are in essence guiding others to solve their own problems, come to their own decisions and/or reach their own goals. They truly are the "guide on the side" (confidant) rather than the "sage from the stage" (expert). Chapters Three and Four in this book have more specific information on developing the tools of asking good questions and listening.

So to become an effective confidant, practice using the tools outlined in this chapter. Learn to:

- **have high expectations of others and communicate those to them;**

- **ask positive, solution-focused questions rather than negative, problem-focused questions;**

- **listen actively to not only the words being said but also to the voice tone and body language**; and

- **become a guide to help others discover their own answers**.

Consider the impact of these tools on your people's productivity. In our workshops we ask participants to make a list of "feeling" words that are generated by a coach who uses these tools in positive ways as compared to a coach who doesn't use them or uses them incorrectly. For example, we have them experience a series of positive, solution-focused questions and then experience a series of negative, problem-focused questions. The list of feelings they generate after this exercise often looks like this:

Feelings associated with the **negative** questions:	Feelings associated with the **positive** questions:
Frustrated	Hopeful
Restricted	Positive
Helpless	Empowered
Interrogated	Engaged
Talked down to	Anticipative
Hopeless	Confident
Disengaged	Partnered with

I then look at the workshop participants and ask them this simple question: "For your people to be the most productive they can be, how do you want them feeling most of the time? Do you want them to feel frustrated, restricted, hopeless and disengaged, or do you want them to feel hopeful, positive, empowered and engaged?" The answer is obvious. The point is made that to be most effective in helping people grow while also getting good results, good managers and coaches use these tools in a positive way. Someone once wisely remarked, "People won't always remember what you do or say, but they will almost always remember how you make them feel."

The next three chapters will help you polish these fundamental skills of an effective coach. As a person who learns to practice using these tools, you might just find yourself on a list someday as a trusted mentor who "saw more in somebody than they saw in themselves." You truly will have become a confidant in the process!

CHAPTER 3

Coaching Fundamental #1:
Asking Good Questions

Name just about any top athlete or performer today, and you will find that each of them employs a coach to help him/her get better at his/her game. And what do they spend their time working on? The answer is the fundamentals. Legendary Green Bay Packers football coach Vince Lombardi was said to have started his football program the same way every year by holding up an object and stating, "Gentlemen, this is a football." Lombardi was starting the year off by reminding the players of the most basic fundamental — the ball itself. The team would then spend a huge amount of time in early practices working on the fundamentals of football — blocking, tackling, passing, catching, etc.

If outstanding professional athletes recognize the need for continual practice in the fundamentals of their game, why is it in the business world that we spend so little time on the fundamentals of developing people? We give lip service to the concept that "our people are our greatest asset," yet few companies do a great job of developing their people. And few managers make the time to "grow their people" because they are so focused on getting results. It's as if we forget that we get results — at least most of the time — through our people.

So what are the fundamentals of coaching? Just as professional football players need to be able to block, tackle, pass and catch, professional coaches need to be able to ask good questions, listen effectively and offer effective feedback.

Coaching Skill #1: Questioning Effectively

The first skill we will examine is how to ask effective questions. Good coaches recognize that "people don't argue with their own data." If they can ask good questions that draw the answers out of the person they are coaching, the team member will be more likely to buy into the solution and take action to do what is needed to achieve the goal. Effective coaches recognize that questions are one of their most important tools in achieving coaching success. They use questions to draw out the team member, and often help him/her discover his/her own answers. Here are three **effective questioning skills:**

A – Asking good questions

P – Pulling out specifics

E – Excavating the hidden meaning

Asking Good Questions

There are two types of questions to use in coaching and communicating with people.

Open-ended questions are designed to get the other person talking and sharing information. They invite the maximum amount of thinking and participation on the part of the other person. By getting the other person involved through asking open-ended questions, buy-in and commitment are usually increased and better results are attained.

Examples of open-ended question starters:

5 W's – "Who…, What…, When…, Where…, Why…"

1 H – "How…"

"Tell me about…"

"Describe for me…"

As the name implies, open-ended questions tend to open people up. They are designed to get the other person talking. "How did it go this morning when you met with that difficult client?" is a good beginning to what might be a productive coaching conversation. As the person starts to share, you can encourage him/her by asking further questions. "What happened next?" or "How did that feel to you when she said that?" are examples of additional open-ended questions. You can also use open-ended question starters by saying something like "Tell me more about her response" or "Please share an example of what you mean by "Our policies are not very customer friendly." By using a statement like this, you are making a request for the person to talk some more.

Closed-ended questions are designed to start to bring the conversation or coaching session to a close, or to get an answer to a specific question. These questions can usually be answered with one word, such as a "yes" or "no." Examples of closed-ended questions include the following:

"Did you read through the statement of ethics and values that we abide by here?"

"Who do you believe would be your best service rep for this job?"

"On what date did we decide to do the conference this year?"

"Which company did you choose to cater the food for this event?"

This combination of open and closed questions gives the coach a large repertoire of tools to begin the coaching process. And to make questions even more effective, coaches should remember to use positive, solution-focused, forward-thinking questions. Avoid negative, problem-focused, backward-thinking questions. We learned about these types of questions in Chapter Two, "The Coach as Confidant."

To revisit that concept briefly, effective questions will start with a "what" or a "how" vs. a "why" or a "who," and they will be forward thinking vs. backward thinking questions. Questions such as "What's wrong?" "Who's fault is it?" and "Why did this happen?" tend to bring about a negative reaction. They are problem focused, looking backward at what happened and who is to blame rather than being focused on a solution. Substitute questions such as "What do you really want in this situation?" and "How do you think you could accomplish that?" These are thinking about positive future outcomes.

Topics Around Which to Ask Questions

Good coaches ask questions around four general topics that correlate to the 4 G coaching model that we outlined in Chapter One. In our model, these four areas are the Good/Goal, the Gap, the Guidance and the Growth. They correlate nicely with the well-known GROW model. In his classic book, *Coaching for Performance,* author John Whitmore suggests asking questions around these four GROW areas:

Goals (the Good and the Goal)

Reality (the Gap)

Options (the Guidance given)

Way forward (actions for continued Growth)

Since all good coaching starts with a goal, the first set of questions should sound something like this:

"What are some things you've achieved in this last quarter?"

"Were these accomplishments in line with your goals for the quarter?"

"What goals are you setting for this next year?"

"What are some ways in which you are living by the values

that we espouse here at XYZ?"

Follow these with questions aimed at inspecting the gap, or checking on reality.

"What's working for you so far?"

"In which area(s) have you exceeded your goals?"

"Where would you like to do better?"

Next, before giving guidance to your team member, ask for his/her opinions on what he/she might be doing. Encourage him/her to think of as many options as possible before offering your own thoughts and advice. This increases the chances that the coachee will accept more personal responsibility for his/her actions.

"What are some things that you think you could be doing to get better results?"

"How might you go about doing even better in this area in the next few months?"

"What would it look like for you to 'kick it up a notch' in terms of your results?"

"What would need to exist for you to achieve the goals you've set for yourself this year?"

Finally, ask a series of questions around the actions the team member is willing to take to grow and move forward.

"So what will be your first steps in moving forward with this idea?"

"How do you see proceeding at this point?"

"In what ways will you take action to accomplish these goals?"

Pulling Out Specifics

Once you have begun the coaching process by getting the team member talking, a second type of questioning tool may be needed. This questioning skill is designed to follow the questions or statements of the other person with additional questions to clarify confusing or vague statements, and/or to get more information. The coach simply follows the statements of the team member with additional questions — both open ended and closed ended — to dig out more information.

Examples of pulling out specifics:

Salesperson: "I'm doing pretty well with my sales interviews; they're going smoothly."

Coach: "What specifically is working for you?" Salesperson: "I'm doing a good job discovering their real needs by asking lots of open-ended questions."

Coach: "Give me an example or two of a specific question that

you find helpful."

There are two cautions to be aware of when you are pulling out specifics:

1. The first caution is to be careful of how you ask the "why" question, because it can elicit defensiveness.

"Why did you do that?" may cause the other person to get edgy or to react in a negative way. It is generally better to substitute a "how" or "what" question instead of a "why" question. For example, instead of asking "Why did you do that?" substitute one of these questions: "How might you have done that differently?" or "What do you think you might have done that would have worked better?"

2. The second caution is to be careful not to turn the pulling out specifics tool into an interrogation. Some people don't mind being asked a lot of questions because they have a behavioral style that also has a need for lots of information. But some dislike going into so much detail (see Chapter Seven for more information on behavior styles), and they may start to feel you are really grilling them. Here are some tips to avoid turning this questioning technique into an interrogation:

- **Get permission to ask questions.** Say something like this: "It's really important for me to fully understand this situation. Would it be okay to ask you a few more questions?"

- **State up front that your purpose is to make sure you have all the information.** Start by saying, "In order for me to help you determine the best course of action, I'm going to need your help in getting all the facts, so I'll probably be asking lots of questions." Then proceed with your questions.

- **Give a short response first before asking another question.** After the team member has made a response, follow it with a comment and question like this: "I can see why you would think that was an unrealistic course of action. What do you think would have been a better way to handle this?"

- **Summarize the previous answer, and then ask the next question.** "So in your mind, you thought you were doing what the company policy says to do. Is that correct?"

Excavating the Hidden Meaning

This skill is designed to determine the feeling behind the words of the team member. It typically involves using a series of statements and questions to the person after he/she has made a comment. The questions used may be a combination of open and closed questions, and they are designed to understand what the person is feeling in addition to what he/she is saying. Often when the feeling is identified, the person can then make a rational decision about what to do next.

This questioning skill ties into the listening skill of empathizing with the team member that we'll be learning about in the next section. Of all the coaching skills we've talked about in this book, this skill is perhaps the most difficult. It requires a very keen sensitivity to people and an ability to "listen beyond the words" to the deeper meaning of the conversation. Learning to use this skill well is a bonus for the coach and the people he/she is coaching.

Here are some examples of statements and questions designed to excavate the hidden meaning:

Coachee: "I am having real difficulty reaching my _____goals this month."

Coach: "It sounds as if you're feeling really frustrated with this challenge — is that correct?"

Coachee: "I'm very frustrated with it."

Coach: "So you're probably willing to try just about anything to get this figured out — would that be true?"

Coachee: "Well, I'll certainly try anything within reason."

Coach: "What kinds of strategies have you tried so far?"

(Listen)

"How has that worked?"

(Listen)

"Have you tried the technique we shared during last week's meeting?"

Coachee: "I'm not really sure that technique works anymore. It seems outdated to me."

Coach: "You are hesitant to use that technique because you believe it is old school — is that correct?"

(Listen)

Coach: "What might be an advantage of using that technique?"

(Listen)

Coach: "Let me encourage you to try that technique, because several of your other team members are having success with it. And here's one more idea…"

By following this line of statements and questions, the coach is uncovering both the thoughts *and* feelings of the coachee, and he/she is more likely to get a positive result.

So the good coach makes use of the first important tool — asking questions effectively. He/she uses an effective combination of open and closed questions, pulls out the specifics of the situation, and excavates the hidden meaning behind the statements of the person being coached.

CHAPTER 4

Coaching Fundamental #2:

Listening Effectively

Good coaches are adept not only at asking effective questions, but also at being effective listeners. In the context of this book, here are the three most important **effective listening skills:**

A –Acknowledging

P – Paraphrasing

E – Empathizing

Acknowledging

To acknowledge while listening is to show the speaker that you have heard him/her and are interested in what is being said. Acknowledgement may be either verbal or nonverbal. These are a few examples:

Saying, "I see!" or "Uh, huh!"

Holding eye contact, smiling

Nodding your head up and down

Although acknowledgement is a simple skill, it is often not done. This is because we are often distracted in our own minds with other pressing issues, or because we really don't care all that much about the speaker's concerns — we're concerned about ourselves. Acknowledgement means that we have to step outside of ourselves and pay attention to the concerns of others. It ensures that you are giving the other person your full attention, and encourages him/her to be candid and share information freely. In essence when you acknowledge someone, either verbally or nonverbally, you are saying, "I care about you!"

Paraphrasing

Most people recognize the skill of paraphrasing as simply restating what you heard the speaker say in your own words. Note that it is not "parrot-phrasing" — you are not simply repeating the speaker's words directly back, but rather rephrasing them in your own words. The purpose of paraphrasing is *not* to show approval or disapproval, but to summarize the content of what was said so as to indicate that you "got the message." Here are some of the benefits of paraphrasing.

Benefits for the listener (coach):

- Allows you to check for understanding of what was said
- Helps you simplify or clarify a confusing statement from the coachee
- Allows you to move the conversation along without seeming impolite

Benefits for the speaker (coachee):

- Encourages them to keep talking

- Shows that you heard and understood them

- Clarifies the points that he/she has made

If a team member says to you, "I was not sure where John was going in the meeting, because he seemed to be just rambling on and on about the Best account," you could follow his/her statement with "So you thought John was not giving clear signals about his intentions." Notice that this summary statement does not show approval or disapproval. You are not agreeing or disagreeing with the team member — you are simply indicating that you heard what was said by restating it in your own words.

As the speaker hears his/her words coming through you, he/she is able to acknowledge that yes, that is what was said and/or he/she is able to clarify the statement. Although this seems as if it might almost be offensive to the speaker, it is really a powerful way to reinforce him/her and show understanding. Good listeners (and good coaches) become adept at using the skill of paraphrasing.

Empathizing

Empathizing is the most difficult of the listening skills that coaches need to learn. It involves listening past the words to the feeling or tone of the message. The purpose of empathizing is to identify with the emotions of the speaker, to let him/her know that you truly can hear how he/she "feels."

As in paraphrasing, it is important not to share your advice or opinions when you are empathizing. You also do not need to agree or disagree with the person's feelings — you are simply "hearing them out." The result of doing this is that you will tend to diffuse some of the emotion the person is feeling and allow him/her to move on to something else. If people continue to gripe or complain, it is often because they have not had their emotions acknowledged. Empathizing will help to solve this problem.

Three Key Steps to Empathizing:

1. **Listen for and identify the emotion(s) being expressed.**

2. **State to the person the emotion you heard and the reason for the emotion.**

3. **Allow the speaker to confirm what you said.**

Here are some examples of statements and questions designed to show empathy with the speaker:

Salesperson: "I'm working really hard but not hitting my numbers. I don't know what else to do!"

Coach: "It can be really frustrating when you are working so hard, and yet the time and effort just doesn't seem to be paying off."

Service Person: "I don't have time to finish all my paperwork!"

Coach: "Doing the paperwork can seem overwhelming when there seems to be so much else to do to meet customer needs."

Employee: "It doesn't seem fair to me that the insurance

company paid all of Melody's hospital bills, but they are only

going to pay 75 percent of mine!"

Coach: "You are unhappy that the insurance company is not

paying for all of your medical bills."

Notice that each of the above examples is stated slightly differently. The following phrases show the different ways to empathize. Remember that you are reflecting back to the speaker both the "feeling" expressed and the reason for the feeling.

"It's _____ (feeling) when _____ (reason)."

"When _____ (reason), you feel _____ (feeling)."

"You're _____ (feeling) because _____ (reason)."

Feeling Words to Use When Empathizing:

POSITIVE FEELINGS		NEGATIVE FEELINGS	
Awesome	Certain	Anxious	Aggravated
Confident	Comfortable	Confused	Concerned
Determined	Delighted	Discouraged	Disappointed
Enthusiastic	Eager	Doubtful	Exasperated
Excited	Fulfilled	Frightened	Frustrated
Glad	Happy	Insecure	Nervous
Hopeful	Important	Overwhelmed	Scared
Pleased	Relaxed	Trapped	Uncertain
Relieved	Secure	Uncomfortable	Unimportant
Surprised	Sure	Unsure	Worried

Simply Understanding People Helps Them Grow

Dr. Carl Rogers said that our greatest power to help other people grow and facilitate change in their lives is by listening to them, understanding them, and giving them unconditional acceptance. Rogers, the father of modern-day nondirective counseling, found that we don't have to try to "change and fix" people, but that if we listen to them nonjudgmentally and accept them as they are, they often get a bigger view of themselves and begin to change on their own.

The listening skills covered in this chapter — acknowledging people, paraphrasing their words and empathizing with their feelings — are three of the most important things you can do to accept another person unconditionally and help him/her grow.

Chapter 5

Coaching Fundamental #3:
Giving Feedback Effectively

Good coaches know how to give effective, high-quality feedback. To provide this type of feedback, the coach must do three things:

1. Know what "good" looks like; be knowledgeable on the subject being coached

2. Create a climate of trust

3. Provide effective, behavior-based feedback

Be Knowledgeable on the Subject

It is important that the coach has a very clear picture of what the values, goals, standards and behaviors are — and makes sure that these are clearly communicated — in order to be an effective coach. As we say in our seminars, "In the absence of a goal or standard, you are not coaching — you are meddling." It is critical that there is a target — a stated outcome, or else the team member does not know to what he/she is being held accountable.

The interesting fact about coaching is that the coach doesn't necessarily have to be the best performer himself/herself but does need to know what "good" looks like in order to be effective in coaching the team member.

To go back to the sports world for a moment, most of us can think of great athletes who tried to become coaches but had little success in that arena. They could perform, but they could not coach others. Yet there are many examples of moderately successful athletes (and even those who may never have made the big leagues) who have become great coaches. The skills needed to perform and the skills needed to coach can be quite different. What is critical for the coach, however, **is the need to know what skills to coach to — and how to hold the performer accountable.**

Vince Lombardi didn't need to be great at passing, kicking, blocking and tackling, but he did need to know the mechanics of those skills to be able to coach his ball players to success. Likewise, good coaches in business need to study and know the necessary skills of the jobs they are asking their people to do.

Create a Climate of Trust

A key element of effective coaching is to create an environment of trust and honesty. This allows both the coach and the coachee to be their real selves — to be authentic — and in turn leads to good results while growing people. A research study at the University of Minnesota identified four key elements of trust. Listed below are the four elements of what we call the **SOAR** trust model:

Straightforwardness

Openness

Acceptance

Reliability

Also listed are some of the corresponding behaviors that cause managers and coaches to exhibit those elements of trust.

Straightforwardness

Being honest; sharing the truth

Clarifying expectations; no hidden agendas

Encouraging creative, ideological conflict

Recognizing and analyzing errors

Willingly confronting one another

Openness

Asking for and giving feedback willingly

Giving team members a sense of the big picture

Having adequate meetings; frequency and quality

Keeping people informed; not having secrets

Sharing feelings as well as facts and data

Acceptance

Allowing emotions and logic to be expressed

Getting input from all on important decisions

Having mutual respect for differences of opinions

Listening to understand, without interrupting

Respecting different roles and expertise

Reliability

Being on time

Having consistent consequences — rewards/punishments

Keeping confidences

Meeting commitments

Taking responsibility

To get a sense of your ability to create trust, take a moment to go through each of the behaviors listed in the SOAR model on the previous page and above. Put a plus sign beside those behaviors that you believe you do well, and a minus sign beside those that you do not do so well. Use a question mark if you are unsure of your ability in a particular area. By counting your plus signs and minus signs as you finish, you'll have a pretty good sense of which of the four SOAR categories are strengths for you, and which are areas you can grow in as a coach.

When all four of these elements are present in a coaching situation, the willingness of the team member to receive feedback is increased greatly. So practice creating trust, and you will find that your results and the growth of your people will SOAR!

Provide Effective, Behavior-Based Feedback

Once you have identified what good looks like and have worked to create a climate of trust with your team members, then the final component to good coaching is giving effective, behavior-based feedback. The word "feedback" originated in the field of cybernetics, which defines closed-loop systems. For example, think of a thermostat on the wall. It gets information (feedback) from the system about changes in the temperature and is then able to change the state of things by turning on the warm air or cool air. Feedback is the data or information in the system regarding its performance. Applied to coaching, feedback serves the same purpose — it supplies information to the performers about how they are doing in meeting their goals, and helps them make the adjustments to hit the target.

In a coaching situation, all feedback should be given with the goal of helping the person grow while getting the needed results.

Behavior-Based Feedback Topics

Before examining how to make feedback effective, let's first look at what type of topics are appropriate for giving feedback. In our coaching seminars, we introduce the concept of the ABC's of coaching in organizational settings. The letter A stands for Attitude, B for Behavior and C for personal Characteristics. We suggest that in most work settings, we should focus on coaching to the Behavior and avoid coaching to Attitudes and personal Characteristics. When we start to coach to Attitudes and personal Characteristics, we cross the fine line between coaching and counseling. And unless we've had training to become a counselor, we generally don't want to go into that arena.

In my seminars, I use this example to make my point. I tell participants that I am going to be back in a moment, and then I walk out of the room. I pick up a roll of masking tape, and then re-enter the room in a rather violent fashion. I swing open the door, and then slam it shut behind me.

I say very loudly and emphatically: "I am so sick and tired of what's going on around here! If you people don't shape up, something bad is going to happen!" As I say these words, I throw the roll of tape to the ground and then slap my hand down on an open table in the room. Of course the participants are startled and taken aback — until I smile and let them know that I am just play-acting. After a few moments, I ask them the following question:

> **"What did you observe in the last few seconds as I came into the room?"**
>
> Responses will vary, but they always include comments like these:
>
> *"You were out of control!"*
>
> *"You were angry — you lost your temper!"*
>
> *"You seemed like you had gone crazy!"*

I then ask the group how many of them enjoy watching crime dramas on television, especially watching the court scenes on these shows. A number of people will raise their hands. I then set up this scenario and ask a question:

"Imagine a courtroom scenario, with a trial taking place. A witness is on the stand, and he makes several statements like this: 'He [the defendant] was out of control; he was very angry.' The defense attorney jumps up at this point and says, 'Objection your honor — speculation on the part of the witness!'"

The question I then ask is this: "What would the judge rule — at least most of the time — in this situation? Would the judge rule that the objection is sustained, or overruled?"

As participants think about it, several will usually say "sustained." And they are correct in their assessment. In other words, the witness cannot use nonspecific language to describe the defendant's behavior. For evidence to be allowed in a court of law, the witness would have to say things like "The defendant was yelling loudly and holding his fists up next to his face" rather than "He was angry and out of control." This would now be acceptable testimony on the part of the witness, because it is *observable* and *specific*!

Finally, I go back to my original question:

> **"So once again, what did you observe a few moments ago about my behavior?"**
>
> Now the group is beginning to understand my point, and the comments include these:
>
> *"You slammed the door behind you as you walked into the room!"*
>
> *"Your voice level was three times higher than it has been today!"*
>
> *"You threw some tape on the floor and slammed your fist on the table!"*

The point has been made. Just as a good witness needs to be specific in describing a defendant's behavior in a court of law, a good coach will be specific in describing a team member's behavior to be effective in a coaching situation!

Most of the time, coaches fall into this trap of commenting on attitudes, demeanor and even character with their feedback. To keep ourselves within the bounds of good coaching, the focus should be on the behavior rather than attitudes and character. Comments such as "You raised your voice volume," "You slammed the door" and "You slapped the table" are more appropriate than "You were angry" or "You were out of control," because they address the specific behavior. This is what we mean by behavior-based feedback.

Having said the above, it is important to note that we do have to coach to some of the more subjective attributes as well as the objective components of business. Some of the subjective topics we can safely coach to include the following:

Alignment with organizational values

Collaboration and teamwork

Communications and listening

Flexibility and adaptability

Honesty and integrity

Openness to change

Personal accountability

The key to coaching to these more subjective measures is to quantify them with specific behaviors. For example, under collaboration and teamwork, we would list the specific behaviors — the things we want team members to do and say — that fit that category. Some of these behaviors might include these: arrives on time to meetings, informs team members of daily activities, and encourages others with personal compliments. When we break these subjective attributes down into specific behaviors or standards, we can observe them and coach to them.

The easier things to coach are the objective measures that we use in business and organizational life such as sales, production goals, cost reductions and so forth. Here are additional examples of the objective components of performance:

Accuracy and completeness

Department goals

Financial measures

Planning effectiveness

Production goals

Sales and service measures

Technical skills and competencies

Widgets manufactured

To Make Feedback Effective, Make Sure It SIPS:

S–Specific (What did you see? What did you hear?)

I – Immediate (within 24 hours if possible)

P–Personal (tailored to the person)

S–Sincere (meant to help the coachee grow and get better results)

Specific Feedback

As discussed earlier in this chapter, it is critical that feedback is specific. It should be based on what the coach was able to observe, meaning what he/she saw or heard. (At times, it may be necessary to give feedback based on the report of other observers, but it is best if the coach can be the observer himself/herself. It is difficult to argue with feedback given by someone who was there to see and hear the behavior.)

Let's use a golf example to illustrate this point. Imagine that you are out golfing, and you've asked a partner to coach you on your shot.

After hitting a ball rather poorly, your partner says: "That was pitiful. You didn't even hit the ball into the fairway!"

How helpful is this feedback? You already knew that it was a poor shot and that you didn't hit the fairway. So you really didn't learn anything new from your partner's comment.

Suppose instead he says: "Just before you swung that time, you dropped your right shoulder. Because of that you sliced the ball. Make sure that you keep your shoulders level when you swing the next time."

Now the feedback is specific. You learned not only what you did poorly (something your partner observed), but also you got a tip on how to do better the next time.

In a business context, it's nice to hear "You did a great job in leading that training session today," but it's not very helpful feedback because it is not specific. Here's an example of specific feedback:

"Juan, I really liked the job you did today as you lead the New Employee Orientation training. You had a nice balance of information and interaction, you kept the class moving and ended on time, and you used PowerPoint effectively — about 35 percent of the time.

"I especially liked how you greeted people as they came in, and then gave them your contact information at the end in case they needed any follow-up information. Way to go, and keep up the good work!"

Now the performer knows what to do the next time he trains a group, because the coach has given specific feedback on things that Juan did and/or said. Make sure your feedback is specifically given on observed behavior — what you saw or heard the performer do or say.

Immediate Feedback

The most helpful feedback is delivered in the moment, or as soon as possible after the performance or incident. All too often, managers wait until the "annual mugging" — the yearly performance review — to let people know what they did well or poorly. But this stale feedback is next to worthless, having lost its context and its relevance. If you have developed a level of trust with your team members , it is a good idea to let them know that you will be giving feedback on their performance on a regular basis as it happens.

Of course you have to recognize that there are times and situations that may require holding feedback for a few minutes or even a few hours. While positive feedback can and should be given in front of others (and therefore may be delivered immediately), corrective feedback should be given in private. So you may have to delay the feedback to find a private spot. Also, it is a good idea for a coach to check his/her attitude before delivering corrective feedback. You may need a period of time to cool off and get your emotions in check if the performer has triggered a negative response in you. Allow some time to pass before giving feedback in that kind of situation. In general, though, it is a good idea to try to deliver the feedback within a 24-hour period, and it is even better if you can do it before the workday interaction ends.

Personal Feedback

Effective coaches (including parents) take into consideration the unique personality of and the needs of the person they are coaching.

They recognize that "what works for one doesn't necessarily work for another!" For example, in dealing with a dominant/directing-style personality, a coach can move more quickly to deal with an issue and provide corrective feedback. The best approach with this type of person is to address the issue immediately in a very straightforward way. The director style person tends to be blunt in his/her conversation and appreciates it when others are that way with him/her. But if the coach is dealing with a supporting-style personality, he/she will want to approach giving corrective feedback in a slower, softer way.

This person needs a little more time to reflect on information and should be approached in a gentler way. To learn more about personality styles and how to coach them effectively, see the section in Chapter Seven on the DISC personality styles model.

The other component of personal feedback is to take into account what else is happening in the person's life outside of work. Good coaches will be aware of the unique life situation of their people and make adjustments in their coaching based on that. For example, in coaching a single parent who has sole responsibility for several children, the coach will look for ways to meet the unique needs of this team member. Perhaps the workday could be adjusted to start at 8:30 and go until 5:00, instead of an 8:00 to 4:30 workday, to accommodate the need to get children off to school. The challenge in all of this is to be fair to all concerned. Each performer must meet the acceptable standards of performance, but there might be ways to make adjustments to meet the personal needs of each one.

Sincere Feedback

It seems obvious to say that feedback should be sincere, but what is not always so obvious is how to make a compliment sincere. One of the best ways to check the sincerity of your feedback is to make sure that you can tell the person "why" you said what you did. "The new sales report you created is terrific. The lay out is easy to follow, and the charts and graphs really help to track the progression of sales. You sure make my job easier when you do good work like this. Thank you, and keep it up." This is an example of feedback that includes a why.

It is a good idea to remind ourselves as coaches occasionally of the true purpose of giving feedback. And that purpose is how we define the coaching process — to grow people while getting results. If we choose to see that as the purpose of our coaching, then we will be giving feedback for the right reasons.

Enjoy the coaching process!

CHAPTER 6

The Coach as Cheerleader:
Praising Good Performance

You are a rare person if you are reading this chapter, because most people think that they do a good job of praising good performance. But research published by the Gallup Organization proves otherwise. In studies where Gallup researchers have interviewed over one million employees, it was determined that the main reason people leave organizations is their immediate manager. The research shows that people don't leave organizations — they leave managers. And one of the main reasons they do is that "managers don't seem to care about me as a person — they don't encourage my development." Gallup's research is famous for identifying the levels of engagement among workers today. Their ongoing research shows the following:

- About 25 percent of America's workforce today is "engaged" in their work - they work with passion.

- Approximately 55 percent of the workforce is "not engaged" - they put their time in but are essentially "checked out".

- About 20 percent of the workforce is "actively disengaged." These workers are actually trying to undermine the efforts of everyone else. They are unhappy, and they are busy acting out their unhappiness.

So what is one of the key contributors to employee engagement? The Gallup study indicates that "supervisors play a crucial role in worker well-being and engagement." And one of the ways that they do this is through praising good performance. Effective supervisors recognize that to be an effective coach, they need to learn how to be a cheerleader.

How to Praise Good Performance

There are three simple steps that coaches can take to be good cheerleaders:

1. First, define what "good" looks like. Make sure to develop a checklist of behaviors that are appropriate for each performer in his/her job.

2. Then, when you see the good behavior, say something. Catch people doing things well — and tell them.

3. Finally, be specific. Tell the team member what he/she did that was good.

Defining What "Good" Looks Like

To illustrate step number one, define what "good" looks like, let me share this example from my family life. A few years ago, my wife and I were struggling with our teenage son Will's impossibly messy behavior. His room was a disaster.

Dresser drawers were left open, clothes were strewn about the room, and his video games were scattered about, as well. His bed was seldom made, and pop cans, and food and candy wrappers were left about the room. As good parents, we tried everything we knew to change this behavior, including rewards and punishment. But one day we realized that we had never really defined for Will what a "clean room" looked like. So we went into Will's bedroom one Saturday morning and told him we were going to help him clean his room. We made the bed up according to our standards, hung certain clothes in the closet, and folded and put into the dresser drawers other clothes. We even showed Will that with just a gentle push, the dresser drawers actually went shut! And we picked up video games, and straightened out his play area.

Then I asked Will to get our Polaroid camera (this was a bit before the digital age). We took a picture of the bed, all made up and looking good. We took a picture of the closet with doors open, showing all the clothes hanging neatly in a row. We even took a picture of the dresser with the drawers shut (and clothes folded neatly therein). Finally, we took a picture of the rearranged and picked-up play area. We then pasted these four pictures on a piece of cardboard. "This," we announced to our son, "is what a clean room looks like! And now, when we ask you to make sure your room is clean, what we mean is that it should look like the pictures."

What we realized in this process is that we had never really defined what "good" looked like for our son. Ask any teenager if his room is clean, and he'll probably respond, "Yes." But the key question is this: "By whose standards is it clean?"

We wanted Will to understand that the room needed to meet our standards; his job was to make sure the room looked like the pictures before he went out to play with his friends. Our job as parents was now much easier, because we had a common definition of what "clean" or "good" looked like.

As coaches, we need to make sure that we have defined what "good" looks like for our employees. Usually this means clarifying the values of the department or organization — the principles or standards by which we agree to operate. This also means that we have agreement on what the major goals are for the department and the employee. What objectives is he/she working to accomplish to move the department and/or organization in the agreed-upon direction? The clearer this picture of "good" is, the more effectively we can coach. While we may not actually take pictures, it is a good idea to write out what behaviors and results are expected in order to give the employee a target to shoot for.

Coaching Effectiveness Grid

As an example of what "good" looks like in an organizational sense, here are 10 characteristics that we ask coaches to rate themselves on in our Coaching for Success workshop. As you read these characteristics, rate yourself on a scale of 1–10 against these good coaching behaviors (1 = terrible, 10 = outstanding).

An effective coach:

a. Communicates the values and goals of the organization or team in an effective way. Leaves no doubt as to what is expected from team members — in values and behavior as well as in performance and results.

1_____10

b. Asks good questions. Uses a mix of both open and closed questions that help team members come up with their own solutions. Uses solution-focused questions instead of problem-focused questions.

1_____10

c. Listens to understand. Makes every effort to seek first to understand the team member's position before stating his/her own position.

1_____10

d. Acknowledges the team member. Uses nonverbal signals, such as nodding and smiling, and uses verbal signals such as "uh-huh" and "I understand" to encourage the team member to keep talking.

1_____10

e. Paraphrases and empathizes. Restates comments made by the team member to confirm understanding, and uses empathizing statements to acknowledge feelings.

1_____10

f. Observes performance. Is attuned to what the team member does and says (seeing and hearing) so that he/she can give feedback on the behavior.

1_____10

g. Cheerleads good performance. Acknowledges the things he/she sees and hears by saying something to the performer, being specific about what he/she liked about the behavior.

1_____10

h. Redirects poor performance. Reminds the team member of the good and goal, makes an observation about his/her current behavior (the problem), and asks him/her to comply with the good and/or the goal (the solution).

1_____10

i. Provides balanced, behavior-based feedback. Comments on the behavior (what he/she can see or hear) vs. the attitudes or personal characteristics of the performer.

1_____10

j. Encourages team members to be their best. Sees more in the team member than he/she sees in himself/herself. Looks for positive strengths, traits and characteristics, and points them out to the team member.

1_____10

Opening Your Mouth to Reinforce Good Behavior

Once there is a set of agreed-upon values, standards and objectives (what "good" looks like), then the coach's job becomes largely that of reinforcing the good behavior and redirecting the poor behavior. In the next chapter we will talk about how to redirect the poor behavior. Here are some ways to reinforce the good behavior.

Each time you catch an employee doing something well, open your mouth and acknowledge the good behavior. While this seems like such an easy thing to do, many managers and coaches admit that they don't do a very good job of it. In our coaching seminars, we ask managers to brainstorm why they think there is not more cheerleading going on in organizations today. Here is a representative list of some of the answers:

1. "We pay people, so why do they also need to be praised?"

2. "I'm too busy to be passing out compliments all day."

3. "It's easier to tell people what they did wrong than what they did right."

4. "If I praise people too much, they might get a big head."

While all of these reasons might have a grain of truth in them, managers who think this way miss one of the most important elements of human nature — the human being's need for appreciation. Harvard professor William James, the "father of modern psychology," said it this way: "The deepest principle of human nature is a craving to be appreciated." Notice that he did not say this is a need, a want or a desire. He said it is a craving. Everyone needs to hear that he/she is doing a good job, at least once in a while.

Let's return to Gallup's research and the reasons people are either engaged or not engaged in their work life. When researchers asked if supervisors focused on their strengths, 77 percent of engaged workers strongly agreed, while only 23 percent of not engaged workers agreed. This was a main factor for a lack of employee engagement — not feeling appreciated!

Make Your Praise Specific

The final key element to being a good cheerleader is to make sure you are specific with your praise. We learned in the previous chapter to give feedback on observable behaviors — the things the performer did or said, rather than on his/her attitudes or personal characteristics. How do you praise specifically? By answering this question:

> **"What did you see or hear — what specific words did the contributor say, or what specific behaviors did he/she display — that are worthy of your praise?"**
>
> Here are two examples:
>
> *"Joe, your extra effort in covering phones today really helped us serve our customers."*
>
> *"Becky, the soft tone of voice you used with that upset customer really helped calm the situation and resolve the problem. Congratulations!"*

Specific praise that reinforces the good behavior is almost always believed and increases the chances that the behavior will continue. General praise is often not believed. Even though it is nice to hear that "you did a good job," most people would much rather be given a specific reason that their performance was good. So, to be an effective cheerleader, remember these three keys:

1. First, define what "good" looks like. Make sure to state the values to be lived by and the goals to be reached, and develop a set of behaviors appropriate for each performer in his/her job.

2. Then, when you see someone achieve a goal or model the good behavior, say something. Catch people doing things well — and tell them what you appreciate about their behavior.

3. Finally, be specific. Tell the team member what he/she did or said that was good.

By doing these three things, you, your team members and the organization will be the beneficiaries.

CHAPTER 7

The Coach as Corrector:

Redirecting Poor Performance

One of the toughest jobs for most coaches is redirecting poor performance. Once the coach has defined what "good" looks like — the values, purpose and objectives of the enterprise — his/her three main tools for accomplishing the good are mentoring (Chapter Two), praise (Chapter Six) and correction. This chapter will focus on the coach's role of correcting or redirecting poor performance.

There are generally two reasons most coaches are poor at correction. They are either too easy on the offender (saying nothing or whitewashing the offense), or too harsh in their correction (not being sensitive to the style and needs of the offender). We call these two extremes the people pleaser or the taskmaster. This chapter will help you determine your tendency to lean toward one or the other and will outline a way of addressing poor performance that avoids these two extremes.

Our tendency toward being a people pleaser or a taskmaster comes out of our natural behavioral style, often called our personality. Most behavioral scientists today believe that our personality is largely genetic — we were born with it.

And most of us who are parents of two or more children would attest to this — our children were different from birth. Their personality was largely established by the time they were coming out of the womb. So let's examine personality, or what we will call "behavioral style," in this chapter and how it contributes to our tendency to be more people focused or more task focused.

In today's workplace, there are three popular models of understanding personality. These are the Myers-Briggs Type Indicator (MBTI), the Social Styles model and the DISC model. While we are fans of any model that will help coaches and team members better understand each other, we use the DISC model in our work. DISC stands for a model of human behavior that looks at **Dominance (D), Influencing (I), Steadiness (S)** and **Conscientiousness (C)** tendencies.

We can explain the DISC model most easily by looking at two continuums of behavior, which we will label "pace" and "focus." We will plot pace on the vertical axis, and focus along the horizontal axis. At the top of the vertical axis are those people who tend to have a faster pace about them. They are often competitive, and express their ideas and beliefs openly and forcefully. They like to tell others what to do. At the bottom of the vertical axis are those people who tend to have a slower pace about them. They tend to be more cooperative, and tend to ask more than tell.

Faster Paced
(Tells)

Slower Paced
(Asks)

Please understand that there is

no right or wrong, good or bad place to be on this scale. Each place is just different. The position each person occupies on the scale depends largely on the traits he/she inherited and on early learning and programming. The horizontal continuum looks at focus. On the left side of the continuum are those whose main focus is tasks. They tend to be more formal in their approach to things and are more controlled in their expression.

On the right side are those whose main focus is people. They tend to be more informal in their approach and more self-expressive. They will often share their emotions freely with those around them, while those on the left of the continuum are not comfortable revealing their deeper feelings.

Task Focused ━━━━━ **People Focused**
(Formal) (Informal)

As in the previous example, there is no one best place to be. This has nothing to do with a person's emotional maturity, abilities or commitments. It has to do with a person's comfort in expressing emotions and priority around task or people. Remember, different does not equal wrong; different just equals different.

By putting these two continuums together, we have now formed a four-quadrant system by which we can characterize behavior. We will call the upper left-hand quadrant the "D" behavior, or Directing. The upper right-hand quadrant is the "I" behavior, or Interacting. The lower right-hand quadrant is "S" behavior, or Supporting, and the lower left-hand quadrant is "C" behavior, or Calculating. Each person is made up of some combination of all four of these behaviors. Most people, however, tend to have a more prominent style and then maybe a secondary and tertiary style.

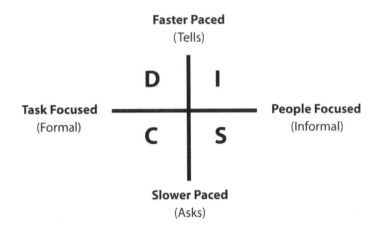

The Directing, Interacting, Supporting and Calculating Styles

A Directing style (Director) is decisive, results-oriented, competitive, independent and strong-willed. Overused, these strengths appear domineering, harsh, tough, impatient, pushy. The Director is motivated by challenges and prefers a fast paced environment. He/she fears being taken advantage of. To increase their effectiveness, Directors need to develop more patience and learn to slow down and socialize. In our coaching model, we call these people taskmasters.

The Interacting style (Interacter) is enthusiastic, persuasive, people oriented, stimulating and talkative. These strengths overused can appear to be undisciplined, excitable, disorganized, manipulative, and reactive. The Interacter is motivated by people contact and an open, accepting environment. They fear a loss of influence. To increase their effectiveness, Interacters need to develop more objectivity, be more organized, and learn to be brief and low key. Interacters tend to be people pleasers in their work as coaches.

The Supporting style (Supporter) is dependable, agreeable, amiable and calm. These strengths overused come across as unsure, insecure, wishy-washy and conforming. The supporter is motivated by stability and prefers an organized, secure environment. To increase their effectiveness, supporters need to be more decisive, say "no" more easily and develop greater comfort with change. Supporters also tend to be people pleasers.

The calculating style (Calculator) is accurate, persistent, cautious and perfectionistic. These strengths, when overused, may appear as critical, picky, judgmental and slow to make decisions. The Calculator is motivated by control and accuracy, and prefers an environment that maintains high standards. Their fear is criticism of their work. Calculators can increase their effectiveness by being more open and tolerant of themselves and others, and by developing an acceptance of realistic limitations. Although Calculators can be quite diplomatic, they also tend toward being taskmasters as coaches.

On a vertical and horizontal axis, we can now go back to our original example of the four-quadrant model (from Chapter One, page 8) and see whether our tendency is to be more people focused or more productivity focused. The DISC behaviors generally will fall into these quadrants. Note that these are tendencies only — training and education can modify behaviors over time. But most people can see themselves in the visual that appears here.

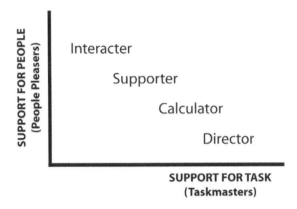

The tendency of Interacters is to be the most people pleasing, followed by Supporters. Directors tend to be the biggest taskmasters, followed by Calculators. Each style has to work to build a better balance, but generally the Interacters need to work the hardest on task focus, and Directors need to work the hardest on people focus. This information usually helps coaches better understand their tendency in their coaching work — to be more people oriented or to be more task oriented. If you choose to discover more about your personality style, check out our website to find out how to take a DISC assessment: **www.MeissEducation.com**. Or phone us at: 952-446-1586

Knowing your style will give you a sense of what is most challenging for you in the balance between people sensitivity and goal achievement (people focus vs. task focus).

Now, let's go back to the original premise of this chapter: Each DISC style will have difficulty correcting people. D's and C's will tend to be more task focused, and therefore may be insensitive to people as they correct them. I's and S's will tend to be more people focused, and therefore may avoid or whitewash the problem. The following process will tend to help all coaching styles be more effective in correcting poor behavior.

How to Correct Poor Performance

After observing poor behavior or performance, follow this process. First, ask the employee if he/she has a few minutes to talk privately. (We call this the "Joan Rivers Rule," so named because of Joan's famous question "Can we talk?")

This question is a signal to the employee that what you want to talk to them about is an important matter. This is not about the weather, the upcoming company party, or the ball game last weekend. This is important stuff.

Once the employee agrees to talk, take him/her to a private place and follow this sequence of conversation:

- **Remind the team member what "good" looks like.** Tell him/her what the goal is — what the behavior is that you want to see modeled or what results you are looking for.

- **Tell the team member specifically what behavior you have seen or heard, and how it missed the mark.** Let him/her know the impact of this negative or poor behavior.

- **Ask for the behavior that you want.**

- **Ask the team member what you can do to help him/her perform the good behavior.**

Use the WWIINN (or Win-Win) Formula

My coaching colleague, Bill Mills, calls this model the WWIINN formula. The model follows this sequence:

W – What do I really, really want?

W – What have I witnessed?

I – What is the impact of this behavior?

I – Use "I" statements as you discuss the behavior.

N – "What I need from you is …."

N – "What do you need from me to be able to do that?"

Using the WWIINN formula creates a win-win for all involved. Let's say that Joe is coming into his job at the call center and getting to his station anywhere between 8:10 and 8:20, when the expected standard is to work from 8:00 to 4:30. An effective coach will recognize that Joe may need some clarification around the standards of being "on time." He/she will talk to Joe and say, "Joe, I need to speak with you about something privately. Do you have a couple of minutes?" (Wait for a response, and if the response is positive, find a private place to talk. If Joe says he can't talk at the moment, agree on a time when you can meet together for a few minutes.)

Then continue by saying: "Joe, please remember that our starting time around here is 8:00 a.m. sharp [what you **want**]. Twice this week you have arrived at your desk from 10 to 20 minutes after our announced start time [what you've **witnessed**]. Your tardiness is affecting the morale of the other team members [the **impact**]. I am disappointed for both you and the other team members when this happens ["I" statement]. I need you to be at your desk, ready to take your first call at 8 a.m., every day. That's what we expect here at XYZ Corporation [**need** from you]. Could you please make that a priority for me?" (Wait for a response.) "What do you need from me to help make that happen [**need** from me]?" "Thanks, Joe — you're an important member of this team, and I look forward to seeing you at your desk, ready to take calls at 8 a.m. each morning."

Although this may seem like a simple conversation, it is not always easy. If done with a balanced interest in Joe's needs and the team's results, the outcome is usually favorable.

Dealing with Bad Habits or Hygiene Issues

Of course, there are some behaviors where a more drastic approach is needed. These are the extreme situations where someone's bad habits or bad hygiene is making the working environment intolerable for other workers — or even customers. Bad breath, improper dress, body odor, a loud or shrill voice, and other such challenges are all too common in the workplace. Yet these difficult situations are usually ignored or handled badly by managers. But most managers agree that these issues have to be addressed, and sooner is usually better than later. Here is the suggested format for handling such situations:

- **Again, start by asking the employee if he/she has a few minutes to talk privately.** Make sure to find a place that is private, where you won't be interrupted.

• **Set the stage by letting the employee know that this will not be an easy conversation.** "Jim, this will probably not be a pleasant conversation for either of us, but I need to talk to you about something" is a pretty good signal to Jim that this is serious.

• **Then use these exact words: "There are times when _____ [state the offending behavior]."** This safe phrase signals that this behavior doesn't happen all the time, but it happens some of the time.

It might sound like this: "There are times when… [choose one]

…your body odor is too noticeable."

… your cursing is upsetting some of our customers."

…your low-cut shirt is distracting to co-workers."

• **After stating the problem, state the solution.** "What I need from you is… [choose one]

…for you to show up tomorrow with no noticeable body odor."

…for you to discontinue cursing in the presence of our customers."

…for you to wear shirts that show no cleavage."

By stating both the problem and the solution, you are letting the employee know exactly what "good" looks like. He/she is then able to respond by either agreeing to change the behavior or by letting you know why he/she may not be able to change (or why he/she thinks he/she can't). If he/she tries to sidetrack you ("Yes, but Charlie also uses swear words around our customers"), make sure to stay on point. Say something like this: "Well, this is not about Charlie, this is about you. And what I need from you is to discontinue cursing in the presence of our customers." Become a broken record (repeating what you want over and over) so that the point is made and the behavior will hopefully change.

Of course these techniques will not always work, and that leads to another role that the coach needs to assume from time to time — the coach as Challenger. That role will be examined in the next chapter. For now, examine your own tendency in correcting behavior — to be either too soft or too hard, too people focused or too task focused. The words and methods listed above will usually help you get the outcomes you want, in a balanced way that builds people while getting top results.

To effectively correct or redirect performance, remember these two methods.

The first is when someone is not exhibiting the type of behavior you want or getting the results you want.

- Remind him/her what "good" looks like, the behavior you want, or what the goal is, the results you are looking for.

- Tell him/her specifically what behavior you have seen or heard and how it missed the mark. Let him/her know the impact of this negative or unproductive behavior.

- Ask for the behavior that you want.

• Ask the team member what you can do to help him/her perform the good behavior.

The second method is when someone is creating a difficult work situation because of bad habits, poor hygiene or other similar situations. In this case, follow this process:

• Start by asking the employee if the employee has a few minutes to talk privately.

• Then use these words: "There are times when _____ [state the offending behavior]." Tell the employee specifically what behavior you have seen or heard and how it missed the mark. Let the employee know the impact of this negative or unproductive behavior

• After stating the problem or offending behavior, state the solution, and ask the team member to abide by it. These suggestions will help you deal with the tough people issues you face in your role as a people developer.

·

CHAPTER 8

Special Situations:
The Coach as Challenger and Facilitator

Coach as Challenger: Confronting Habitually Poor Performance

When an employee has had several chances to correct his/her poor performance or inappropriate behavior and he/she has not done so, the coach needs to confront the behavior immediately. This employee is headed down a dead-end road, and it would be unfair to the organization and the other employees to allow him/her to continue. Some would argue that this role of "challenging" or confronting the employee takes the manager out of the context of being a coach, because there is little attempt to help the employee grow. We'll say a bit more about that in a moment. In truth, this role does put more emphasis on task accomplishment. The goals are not being achieved, or the inappropriate behavior is leading to other unwanted outcomes, and because coaching is a balance between helping employees grow and getting outstanding results, the emphasis here shifts to the results side of the scale.

There is another way of looking at this, however. In many ways, it is also unfair to the employee to allow him/her to continue on this unproductive path. The manager is probably doing this person a favor by confronting these performance issues.

One outcome of this choice is that the performance issues will be resolved, and the employee may keep his/her job. That would certainly be a good result for the employee.

The other outcome is that the employee could be encouraged to leave the company, or he/she may choose to quit of his/her own volition. This choice is also often a good one for the employee, because it provides an opportunity for finding work that is more suited to his/her skills and interests, and/or it allows an employee to find a working environment that may be more to his/her liking. In either case, the argument could be made that in this "challenger" role, the manager is really acting like a coach. There is still an implied outcome of growth for the employee, even though the manager focuses more on the goal achievement side of the equation.

Let's look at the way to make this role of the coach as challenger work most effectively. The first step for a coach about to embark on this role is to become intimately familiar with the organization's human resources (HR) policies. Most organizations today have a standard set of practices for how to discipline and eventually release an employee. The process usually includes a verbal warning (or two) to the employee, which is documented in the files. If the unacceptable behavior continues, there is usually a written warning given, again documented and filed. And then after a certain amount of time, the employee may be legally terminated.

Contracting for Consequences

To start this process, the coach should use the old "contracting for consequences" approach. This approach begins with a statement: "If this _____ [offending behavior] continues, then _____ [this will happen]."

For example, "Joe, if you show up late for work one more time, then I will be giving you a verbal warning." Or, "Patricia, if you are overheard using the __ word with a customer again, I will be giving you a written warning." Or, "Pedro, if you are caught padding your expense account again, you will be released." These statements are effective because they mention the offending behavior and let the employee know specifically what the consequences will be if the behavior continues.

So after attempting to redirect the employee several times with no apparent success (because the behavior has continued), the challenger process goes like this:

1. Ask to meet privately with the employee.

2. Remind the employee what "good" looks like and what the goal is.

3. State the "If ... then" phrase: "If _____ [the behavior] continues, then _____ [this will be the consequence]."

4. Ask the employee to repeat what he/she heard, for clarification.

5. Remind him/her that the outcome will be up to him/her.

This process is usually effective with the employee who may really want to succeed but has somehow not recognized the seriousness of his/her misbehavior or missing the target goals. Once employees are confronted with the "if/then" phrase, they recognize that the coach is really serious, and that they have a choice to make. The responsibility now rests on their shoulders.

The One Who Is Most Committed Wins

This role of a coach allows the manager to also prove the maxim that in coaching (or parenting), "The one who is most committed wins." A great example of this is the one we see played out in everyday life with parents and children. See if you can relate to this example.

A young family is in a restaurant where you've gone for dinner. During the course of the meal, a young child becomes upset about something. She either wants something she can't have, or she is unhappy about being asked to eat something she doesn't want. The child begins fussing, crying and making a scene. One of the adults scolds the child.

Parent: "Lily, if you don't eat your beans, you can't have any dessert."

Child (fussing): "I want some ice cream."

Parent: "You aren't going to get any if you don't finish your food."

Child: (now screaming): But I want some ice cream!"

Sometimes this back-and-forth banter will go on for a while.

If the parent is more committed to his/her outcome, the child will either finish eating and then get some ice cream, or the child will not be rewarded with the dessert. However, *if* the child is more committed to his/her outcome, the parent will often give in and order the ice cream. Children quickly learn if parents are really committed to their outcomes, or if by making a scene, the child can get the outcome he/she wants. Employees are often a lot like that child. They will test a coach to see if he/she is really committed to their outcomes, or if he/she is just blowing smoke. The one who is most committed will win — almost all of the time!

Try a Decision-Making Leave

In his book Discipline Without Punishment, author Dick Grote suggests another technique that works well for habitually poor performance. This is basically the last step a manager or leader would employ when a team member continually performs poorly after being coached and challenged repeatedly.

The concept is that the employee is asked to take a day away from work (with full pay) to make a decision to:

- solve the performance problem and make a commitment to good performance in every area of his/her job, or
- resign from his/her position within the company.

The day is paid so that the employee can completely focus on his/her decision and not worry about income. If the employee chooses to remain at the company and improve performance, and later another situation arises in which disciplinary action is necessary, the employee is then terminated. This outcome needs to be made clear before the employee takes his/her decision-making leave and makes a final decision. If the employee chooses to resign from the position, the manager needs to consider preparing a letter that specifies the terms of the resignation and answers all questions about benefits, pay, reference letters, etc.

Good coaches keep the outcomes of employee behavior directly on the employee, and therefore nurture personal responsibility. It's all a part of growing people while getting results. Remember, "The one who is most committed wins!"

The Coach as Facilitator: Resolving Conflicts between Others

The other special situation that coaches (and parents) often encounter is when two or more employees (or kids) get crossways with each other, and then one comes to the supervisor or parent to resolve the differences. The message is that "we don't know how to solve this conflict between us, so would you please resolve it for us?" What they are doing is transferring the responsibility for the situation from themselves to the supervisor or parent. If not handled properly, this can become a lose-lose proposition. To handle this situation appropriately, the supervisor or parent needs to become a facilitator.

The word "facilitate" comes from the French word "facile," and means "to make easy." The goal of a manager, parent or "coach" in this situation is to help the two concerned parties facilitate their own solution. So in this sense, the coach becomes a facilitator.

Good coaches realize that they must not take the responsibility on their own shoulders to solve the problem (unless it is a parent working with very young children), but that they need to help the two people come up with their own solution. They keep the burden of responsibility on the shoulders of the other two, while agreeing to help facilitate a solution.

Let's say employee A (Al) has a disagreement with employee B (Bonita). Al comes to your office complaining about Bonita and asks you to help resolve the issue.

As a coach, your first line of defense is to ask Al if he has talked to Bonita about this situation. Encourage him to have a face-to-face conversation with Bonita and see if the two of them can work things out.

Once you are satisfied that the two of them have met and discussed things but were not able to resolve their differences, you may then decide to become a facilitator in the situation.

The methodology for this facilitation process is very specific and detailed. There are five key steps that if executed well, will usually lead to a mutually satisfying resolution. Let's look at each step separately, and then put them all together at the end.

Step One is to find neutral ground on which to conduct your meeting. Do not meet at either of the employee's offices or workstations. And if possible, get out of your office, also. Find a conference room or some other room that is totally enclosed and private. You want all parties involved to feel that this meeting will be confidential.

Ask Al and Bonita to sit face to face with each other, while you sit off to the side.

Step Two is to establish ground rules. Greet the two participants and tell them the purpose of the meeting. In the example given above, you would explain to Bonita that Al had come to you with a challenge.

You encouraged him to have the two of you meet, and it appears that the situation is still not totally resolved. Tell them that the purpose of this meeting is for you to facilitate a resolution between the two of them.

Explain the two key ground rules for the discussion:

1. Only one person should speak at a time.

2. Each person should try to share "facts" only — what he/she saw or heard.

Step Three is to manage the process. Begin by asking the originating party (Al in this case) to share his concern. Once Al has finished speaking, give Bonita a chance to share her perspective on the situation.

During the conversation, remain neutral as best you can, and follow the ground rules mentioned above (you'll probably have to keep reminding them "facts only," and "only one person speaking at a time"). From time to time, summarize the issues as you've heard them.

Step Four is to assume the role of a confidant. Ask solution-focused questions during the discussion, looking for answers or compromises to the situation. Some examples of these kinds of questions include "What do you think might work in this situation?" "How do you see this working out?" and "When do you think you could start this new procedure?" (See Chapter Two, "The Coach as Confidant," for more ideas on solution-focused questions.)

Help the two parties come to a mutually agreeable resolution. Be careful not to force any solution on either party, as this usually leads to lack of buy-in on their part.

Step Five is to agree to revisit the situation. It usually sounds something like this: "Al and Bonita, I'm pleased that you've come to an agreed-upon solution to this situation. I'd like for us to meet back in this same room at the same time next week, just for a checkup on how it's going.

"Then if we need to make any adjustments, we can do so and keep this thing moving positively forward. Thank you — I'll see you both here next week." This impending meeting usually causes both Al and Bonita to work hard to make the solution work, because they know they will be held accountable the following week.

So in summary, the steps of the process are as follows:

1. Find neutral ground.

2. Establish ground rules.

>One person speaking at a time

>Share "facts" only — What did they see or hear?

3.Manage the process.

>Remain neutral

>Follow the ground rules

>Summarize the issues

4. Assume the role of a confidant, by asking solution-focused questions.

5. Agree to revisit the solution in a week or so.

Always be careful to keep the responsibility for working out the problems on the shoulders of the two participants. Each or both of them will want to shift the burden to your shoulders, but a skilled coach (and parent) will avoid this situation. By keeping the responsibility for resolution on their shoulders, you are teaching them a process for conflict resolution that will help them the rest of their lives. By doing this, you are fulfilling the job of a good coach — building people, while getting results!

CHAPTER 9

Putting It All Together

We began chapter one of this book talking about the shortage of skilled workers to fill the jobs in organizations today. Finding the right people with the right skills to fill important jobs has become one of the most pressing challenges of recruiters. To help fill this gap for skilled workers, successful organizations are doing everything they can to help current employees develop to their full potential. They are also working hard to keep their best employees. That is why it is so important to teach managers to coach effectively, as managers have a huge impact on the success and morale of their employees.

We have described coaching as "a series of meaningful conversations designed to grow people while getting great results". Invariably, managers ask the question: "How often should I have these meaningful conversations?" Although there is no one "right" answer to this question, the best answer is to have them often enough to ensure the growth of the employee and the accomplishment of great results. In the early stages of development and/or in the beginning part of working on new goals, it might be important to hold coaching conversations weekly or bi-weekly. For more advanced performers, it may be appropriate to meet once a month. To stay connected to your people, it is recommended to meet at least bi-monthly or quarterly.

Coaching Best Practices

Here are some best practices for coaching conversations, followed by a variety of resource sheets to help you coach more effectively:

See your coachee for what he/she could become.

Prepare your coachee for the sessions by giving him/her the Sample Memo: Some Ideas About Coaching (page 87). Talk about the purpose of the sessions in advance and how to prepare for them.

Plan your coaching session by filling out a Pre-Coaching Preparation Form (page 89). Remember that "it's more important for you to think about what you're going to ask than what you're going to say".

Use the enclosed Sample Coaching Questions sheet (page 86) to work on developing your questions. Make your questions as relevant to your coachee as possible.

Begin the coaching session in a positive way. Create the most confidential, positive, and safe environment (both physically and psychologically) that you can.

Work with your coachee on one area at a time. Focus on one or two goals that are important to the coachee and his/her job performance.

Ask him/her questions about how they are doing in achieving the goal. Spend most of your time questioning and listening rather than dominating or giving advice.

Keep the responsibility for goal-achievement on your coachee's shoulders. Be careful to avoid taking on tasks or responsibilities that should be his/her own.

Praise any progress your coachee makes that you observe or hear about. Make sure your praise is specific, immediate and personal.

Redirect any behaviors that need to be addressed. Remember that "what you allow, you teach", so confront and redirect those behaviors that are not productive.

Keep a balance between goal achievement (getting results) and personal and professional growth (growing the coachee).

Separate the worth of your coachee from his/her actions. Value the person even when you cannot value his/her behaviors.

Remember: "Coaching means you care!"

Keep your coaching sessions to one hour or less, and hold them as frequently as it makes sense for the two of you (weekly, bi-weekly, monthly, quarterly).

Sample Coaching Questions

What questions do you have about our coaching sessions?

What are you thinking about these sessions? How do you feel about doing them?

What would make these sessions the most productive for you?

What is a goal that you are currently working on?

How realistic do you think this goal is?

How successful have you been in achieving your goal?

What kinds of actions/behaviors have helped you in accomplishing your goal?

What new knowledge might you need to accomplish your goals?

What are some actions/behaviors you could develop that would help you do even better?

What new work habits might it take to reach your goals?

When might you begin implementing the new knowledge/actions/work habits?

Who might be a resource for you in achieving your goals?

How might I assist you in the accomplishment of your goals?

What areas of personal/professional growth would be helpful to you?

What kinds of rewards are **you** looking to enjoy as you reach your goals?

Sample Memo

Preparing Your Coachee

Here is a sample memo you can customize to help prepare your coachee for the coaching experience. Employee's often question manager's motives for wanting to meet with them, so reviewing this memo with your coachee will help you set up your sessions for maximum success

Some Ideas about Coaching

I would like to begin holding some coaching sessions with you. A coaching session is a positive growth experience that I have recently been trained to conduct. The purpose of the sessions is to help you reach goals that you have in your job, and to help you grow as a person. Our time together is designed to be a very productive and positive experience. As we work together, I will be learning and growing as well. We can decide together on the frequency of our meetings. Sessions will last about one hour, and we can hold them in a private place in our organization.

How to Prepare for Our Coaching Sessions

Please plan to come prepared to our first session with some well-thought out goals for yourself and your job. These should be relatively short-term goals — between 6 months and one year. The goals should relate to your productivity, job performance, career advancement — anything that relates to the work you do here.

Make your goals SMART goals. They should be:

S*pecific:* *A statement of an end result that you'd like to achieve that is …*

M*easureable:* *Include some metrics with the goal, and make sure it is …*

A*chievable:* *Set your goal just out of reach, not out of sight, and make it …*

R*elevant:* *Make sure the goal fits you and your job, and also make it …*

T*imed:* *Give your goal a deadline or some time frame.*

Some Examples of SMART Goals:

- *My goal is to have a fully documented, 10+ page research report written and submitted to marketing by _____.*

- *My goal is to sell $_____ of product each month by _____.*

- *My goal is to service my customers with service and a smile, achieving a _____% satisfaction rating by _____.*

A Few More Thoughts About Your Coaching Sessions

Although I will be leading our discussions, you will be doing most of the talking. I will be asking you questions about your goals, how you are doing in achieving them, and ways that I might be of support to you. Although I will be available for advice and input, for the most part I will be challenging you to find your own answers. These should be meaningful conversations.

I look forward to our coaching sessions and trust you will find them helpful and productive!

Pre-Coaching Preparation Form

To help you prepare for your coaching conversations, take some time to plan the key elements of your approach. Shown here is a sample Coaching Preparation sheet. Use it to prepare yourself each time you are about to hold a coaching conversation.

Good/Goal:

What are this person's goals? What goals would I like this person to achieve?

_____

_____

_____

What Knowledge, Skills and Attitudes (behaviors) would I like this person to work on?

_____

_____

_____

Gap:

What gaps have I observed in this person's performance or behavior (+ and – gaps)?

_____

_____

_____

Guidance:

What solution-focused questions can I ask to get this person discovering his/her own solutions?

_____

_____

_____

_____

_____

_____

_____

_____

_____

What kind of guidance will I give in the form of:

Cheerleading:

_____

_____

Mentoring:

_____

_____

Redirecting:

_____

_____

Challenging:

_____

_____

Growth:

What adjustments will I make in my coaching based on the coachee's:

Behavioral style:

_____

_____

Generational uniqueness:

_____

_____

Life situations:

_____

_____

_____

Coaching: A Meaningful Conversation

(Use the following template as a guide as you hold your coaching conversations.)

Introduction:

_____

_____

_____

Good/Goal:

Ask/Listen: What goal(s) are you currently working on?

_____

_____

Ask/Listen: What behaviors are you developing to achieve this goal?

_____

_____

Ask additional coaching questions, as appropriate. (Listen)

_____

_____

Suggest: Here is a goal I'd like you to be working on (if different from his/her goal):

_____

_____

Gap:

Ask/Listen: How do you think you are doing in achieving the goal?

_____

_____

Ask/Listen:

What barriers are currently keeping you from achieving the goal?

_____

_____

Suggest:

Here is something I've observed that seems to be a challenge in this area:

_____

_____

Guidance:

Provide feedback in one of the following ways:

Cheerlead and encourage the good performance (coach as cheerleader)

Mentor and teach in the areas that need development (coach as confidant)

Re-direct and focus any behavior that needs to change (coach as corrector)

Challenge and confront any dead-end behaviors (coach as challenger)

_____

_____

_____

_____

Growth:

Encourage the growth of the coachee through praising and challenging his/her efforts

Recognize the DISC behavioral style of the coachee and adapt to that style

Acknowledge the generational differences between you and coach accordingly

Discover difficult life situations of the coachee and adapt as appropriate

Coaching Skills Behavioral Checklist

Use the following form to assess your own coaching skills. This form is designed for someone to observe your behaviors as a coach, and give you feedback on your coaching performance.

Questioning   **Yes No N/A**

The coach asked mostly open-ended questions?

Most open-ended questions began with a "what", "when", or "how"?

The coach asked appropriate closed-ended questions?

The coach dug for specifics by asking a series of questions?

The coach avoided the appearance of interrogating the employee?

The coach attempted to excavate the hidden meaning?

Listening   **Yes No N/A**

The coach acknowledged the employee verbally ("I see", "interesting," etc.)?

The coach acknowledged the employee non-verbally (head nod, smile, etc.)?

The coach paraphrased the employee's comments?

The coach utilized an empathizing statement?

The coach correctly identified the feelings of the employee?

Giving Feedback   Yes   No   N/A

The coach focused on observable behaviors vs. attitudes or
personal characteristics?

The coach was specific, telling the employee what he/she did
and/or said?

The coach gave feedback immediately, as appropriate?

The coach made the feedback personal, taking into account the
employee's:

> Behavioral style
>
> Generational uniqueness
>
> Life situation

List a strength this coach has that he/she should continue and build
on:

_____

_____

_____

List an area in which this coach could do better and improve:

_____

_____

_____

Comments:

_____

_____

_____

Managers as Coaches, Not Bosses

All of us struggle from time to time with control issues. We like to be in charge. We enjoy telling others what to do. We want to persuade others to do what we want them to do. And while controlling others is not necessarily right or wrong, it is ineffective in creating trusting, productive relationships. An old axiom sums this up best: "Someone convinced against their will is of the same opinion still!" To get buy-in and engagement from team members, good coaches will keep in mind the true intention of coaching — to help grow the person while also getting the results needed. In the long run, this almost always works better than trying to manipulate and control someone.

Closing the Loop

This premise takes us back to our opening chapter. Bosses have a belief that they can't trust people to do a good job, so they find ways to "boss people around." Controlling others is the key strategy of a manager locked into the paradigm of being the boss. Those leaders and managers who can shift their focus to that of being a coach, however, find ways to build a climate of trust and esprit de corps, creating an environment where team members are free to contribute in their own unique ways and to be their best. This kind of a coaching environment accomplishes the ultimate goal of coaching — to grow people while getting results.

Since I used my son as an example of a coaching principle, let me close the book by sharing an experience in my daughter's life. When Katherine was about five years old, we had just moved to a new home in the western suburbs of Minneapolis. Because it was just a two-bedroom home and we now had a daughter and a son, we began the process of building another bedroom in the basement.

One evening we had some good friends of ours over for dinner. Mark and Polly were Katherine's godparents, so she called them Uncle Mark and Aunt Polly. After dinner, I took Mark downstairs to show him the progress we were making on constructing the new bedroom.

Unbeknown to us, Katherine had followed us downstairs as well. Suddenly she was pulling on Mark's pant leg and saying, "Uncle Mark, Uncle Mark!" As Mark and I looked down to acknowledge Katherine, she looked up with the widest eyes and biggest smile and said, "Uncle Mark, this is my room!"

What I realized was that what Katherine saw in that room was not the same thing that Mark and I saw at that moment. She didn't see just a concrete floor with concrete block walls and a few 2x4-foot studs sticking up out of the floor. What Katherine saw was the completed bedroom: flowered wallpaper on the walls, her furniture arranged neatly in the room, her dolls lined up on her pretty pink bedspread, and her personal items around the room. What Katherine saw in that room was the finished product!

I like to use that example to share with coaches what our goal might be in coaching, which is to not see the people you coach as they are now, but to see them as they might be. This echoes the thought by the German author and poet Goethe, who said, "Treat people as if they are what they ought to be, and you help them become what they are capable of being."

As we take on this important role of growing people while getting results, the rewards include much more than just getting good results. They include the incredible psychic reward of seeing people become all they are capable of being. And that reward is priceless!

Happy Coaching!

Coach Roles and Coaching Models Summary

The 4 G Coaching Model

To help people become great coaches, remember the 4 G coaching model.

1. **Good/Goal**

2. **Gap**

3. **Guidance**

4. **Growth**

The Differences Between Coaching And Bossing

Coaching	vs.	Bossing:
Leading and inspiring		Dictating and controlling
Asking and listening		Telling and directing
Seeks the answers		Knows the answers
Goal driven		Process driven
Future oriented		Past/present oriented
Customer/people focused		Systems/process focused
Setting direction		Setting plans and rules
Empowering		Controlling
Looks for solutions		Looks for problems/blame
Seeing people as they could be		Seeing people as they are

The Coach as Confidant

The tools of a coach as confidant include these:

- **Having high expectations of others — and communicating those to them**

- **Asking positive, solution-focused questions rather than negative, problem-focused questions:**

Solution-Focused Questions	vs. Problem-Focused Questions
What do you really want?	What's wrong?
When do you want it?	Why did this happen?
How might you get it?	Whose fault is this?
What resources are available?	Why can't you succeed?

Feelings associated with the solution-focused questions include these:

Hopeful

Positive

Empowered

Engaged

Anticipative

Confident

Partnered with

• **Listening actively to not only the words being said, but also to the voice tone and body language**

• **Becoming a guide to help others discover their own answers**

Three Fundamental Coaching Skills:

Become a Coaching APE

1. Effective questioning skills:

A – Asking good questions

P – Pulling out specifics

E – Excavating the hidden meaning

2. Effective listening skills:

A – Acknowledging

P – Paraphrasing

E – Empathizing

3. Effective feedback skills:

A – Agreeing on what "good" looks like; being knowledgeable about the subject being coached

P – Providing a climate of trust

E – Effectively delivering behavior-based feedback

The Soar Trust Model

Straightforwardness

Being honest; sharing the truth

Clarifying expectations; no hidden agendas

Encouraging creative, ideological conflict

Recognizing and analyzing errors

Willingly confronting one another

Openness

Asking for and giving feedback willingly

Giving team members a sense of the big picture

Having adequate meetings; frequency and quality

Keeping people informed; not having secrets

Sharing feelings as well as facts and data

Acceptance

Allowing emotions and logic to be expressed

Getting input from all on important decisions

Having mutual respect for differences of opinions

Listening to understand, without interrupting

Respecting different roles and expertise

Reliability

Being on time

Having consistent consequences — rewards/punishments

Keeping confidences

Meeting commitments

Taking responsibility

Effective Feedback Sips

To make feedback effective, make sure it SIPS, being:

S – Specific

(What did you see? What did you hear?)

I – Immediate

(within 24 hours if possible)

P – Personal

(tailored to the person)

S – Sincere

(meant to help the coachee grow/get better results)

The Coach as Cheerleader:
Praising Good Performance

To be an effective cheerleader, remember these three keys:

1. First, define what "good" looks like. Make sure to state the values to be lived by and the goals to be reached, and develop a set of behaviors that is appropriate for each performer in his/her job.

2. Then, when you see someone achieve a goal or model the good behavior, say something. Catch people doing things well — and tell them what you appreciate about their behavior.

3. Finally, be specific. Tell the team member what he/she did or said that was good.

The Coach as Corrector:

Correcting (Redirecting) Poor Performance

1. Remind him/her what "good" looks like, the behavior you want, or what the goal is, the results you are looking for.

2. Tell him/her specifically what behavior you have seen or heard, and how it missed the mark. Let him/her know the impact of this negative or unproductive behavior.

3. Ask for the behavior that you want.

4. Ask the team member what you can do to help him/her perform the good behavior.

The Coach as Corrector:

Addressing Bad Habits, Poor Hygiene, Etc.

1. **Start by asking the employee if he/she has a few minutes to talk privately.**

2. **Set the stage by letting the employee know that this will not be an easy conversation.** "Jim, this will probably not be a pleasant conversation for either of us."

3. **Then use these words:** "There are times when _____ [state the offending behavior]."

4. **After stating the problem or offending behavior, state the solution, and ask the team member to abide by it.**

The Coach as Challenger:

Confronting Poor Performance

1. Ask to meet privately with the employee.

2. Remind the employee what "good" looks like and what the goal is.

3. State the "If ... then" phrase: "If _____ [the behavior] continues, then _____ [this will be the consequence]."

4. Ask the employee to repeat what he/she heard, for clarification.

5. Remind him/her that the outcome will be up to him/her.

The Coach as Facilitator:

Resolving Issues Between Employees

To facilitate conflict between two employees at odds with each other, the correct response is to become a facilitator and follow these steps.

1. Find neutral ground.

2. Establish ground rules.

One person speaking at a time

Share "facts" only — What did they see or hear?

3.Manage the process.

Remain neutral

Follow the ground rules

Summarize the issues

4. Assume the role of a confidant, by asking solution-focused questions.

5. Agree to revisit the solution in a week or so.

Bibliography

The following books have been helpful in constructing the content for this book on coaching. The pre-1990 titles are classic books that have stood the test of time and would be helpful for anyone dealing with coaching and people situations.

Allessandra, Tony and O'Connor, Michael – *People Smarts,* Pfeiffer & Company, 1994

Ayers, Keith – *Engagement Is Not Enough,* Advantage Media Group, 2006

Blanchard, Ken and Johnson, Spencer – *The One-Minute Manager,* William Morrow and Company, 1982

Bolton, Robert – *People Skills,* Prentice Hall, 1986

Carnegie, Dale – *How to Win Friends and Influence People,* Simon and Schuster, 1936

Collins, Jim – *Good to Great,* Harper Collins Publishing, 2001

Cottrell, David and Layton, Mark – *The Manager's Coaching Handbook,* Cornerstone Leadership Institute, 2002

Crane, Thomas – *The Heart of Coaching,* FTA Press, 2001

Gallwey, Timothy – *The Inner Game of Work,* Texere, 2000

Grote, Dick – *Discipline Without Punishment,* American Management Association, 1995

Homan, Madeleine, and Miller, Linda – *Coaching in Organizations,* John Wiley and Sons, 2008

Media Partners Corporation – *The Practical Coach,* DVD and book, 1997

Mills, Bill – *Breakthrough: The Power of Conscious Conversation,* Beaver's Pond Press, 2003

Warren, Arnie – *The Great Connection,* Pallium Books, 1997

Whitmore, John – *Coaching for Performance, Nicholas Brealey Publishing,* 1992

Made in the USA
San Bernardino, CA
04 April 2015